MW01491347

Copyright © 2(

Compiled and written by Deborah ...

Illustrator, Toney Designz

Editor, Deborah Williams

Publisher, Quoniam Global Communications (QGC)

Library of Congress Control Number: 2024924841

Summary: Testimonials of women who exemplify what it means to mother children through faith in God.

ISBN 978-0-984028993 – paperback

ISBN 978-0-984028962 – eBook

ISBN 978-0-984028986 – audio book

First published in 2025
by Quoniam Global Communications.
Printed and published in the
United States of America.

Mothers On a Mission

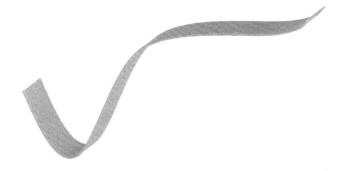

DEDICATION

I dedicate this book to my beloved mother, Maldotha Williams - the woman who introduced me to the Lord, His word and His way, the mother who loves without measure, the woman who lives the call of motherhood out to the fullest.

Beatriz Cumberbatch, "A consistent, persistent, and when need be resistant mother is necessary for a child's proper development."

Vonnie Heywood & Velma Hamilton, "We would never favor one of our children over the other."

Maldotha Williams, "I aligned my parenting with GOD's word."

Rossina Zacarias, "We let our time together and moments of reflection melt the stress away."

Deborah Williams, "Whenever I got overwhelmed with thoughts of inadequacy and my inability… I was comforted by the reminder of God's empowering grace and continued provision."

Carolyn Belle, "Mothers learn as we go."

"As the head of my life, GOD is free to demonstrate His loving nature through me to my children, husband, and to all others I encounter."

CONTENTS

The Author

Deborah Williams is a mother, writer, and writing coach to intellectually disabled youth and adults. She earned a Bachelor of Science in Sociology from Baruch College, City University of New York. Deborah successfully navigated her career through Corporate America before embracing her calling to write.

As a woman of faith, Deborah writes to encourage spiritual growth, to ignite the conscious mind, and stimulate positive personal and social change.

Her first endeavor as a published author was *Wisdom for the Excelling Life*, a repository of testimonials and morsels of life changing wisdom. She subsequently authored *Man-U-Script: the ethos of manhood*, and the *Kids for President* series for children. Deborah is also the creator and editor of MoorBrothers.com blog, which serves as a forum where in black men discourse the nuances of manhood.

Commitment,
Persistence,
Perseverance

Beatriz

I enjoyed motherhood. Now that I'm a grandmother, I enjoy it even more. As a mother I was committed to my children's development, excellence, and productivity. I believe that a consistent, persistent, and when need be resistant mother is necessary for a child's proper development. The most important ingredient that my husband and I used in raising our children was love. We applied it in all that we did, especially when it came time for discipline.

We had our two children in the latter half of the 1960s, when we were still residing in our native Panama. My husband was born in the U.S. controlled Panama Canal Zone which made him eligible to enlist in the U.S. Military. Soon after the birth of our second child he enlisted and was sent to fight in Vietnam, leaving the kids and I in our home in the Canal Zone. I would go often to the Catholic Church to pray for his safe return. Life was difficult because of how much we missed him.

We once went months without any communication, so I prayed and went to the Red Cross to ask them to find him. GOD heard and answered my prayers. He came home safe and sound in 1969 after one year of service in Vietnam.

In June of 1970, not long after his return, I traveled to the U.S. to prepare to move my family there. Life in New York without my children was unbearable, so my stay was brief. I cried day and night for them. Thanks to my daughter's godmother who worked as an operator at the telegraph company in Panama, I was able to have regular conversations with my husband and children. By December of that same year the longing for my children drove me back to Panama. I just couldn't take living without them. The next time I went to New York was in 1971 when we migrated to the United States as a family.

We lacked nothing as we settled into our Brooklyn apartment on Pennsylvania Avenue. My children had everything they needed and just about anything they wanted. They had a stable family. My husband always made sure that we were secure. I knew I didn't need to work but I wanted to for my children's sake. I wanted to prepare for their future. Somehow, I was able to convince my husband of my reason, and then I went out to work.

When our daughter reached school age, we had to decide between purchasing a home and giving her a quality parochial school education. We opted for private school education for both children. My husband covered our daughter's tuition elementary through college, and my income covered our son's.

Like any family we had our ups downs - lumps and bumps, but we forged ahead as a unit with my husband and I protecting our children, holding the reins, and making wise decisions for them until they were able to take the reins themselves. We were persistent in supporting their growth, consistent with discipline. And Me, I was sometimes found protecting them with the ferocity of a lioness.

One time when my son was in elementary school a little boy hit him repeatedly. When my Michael got tired of being bullied he hit the boy back. To top that, the boy's father took it upon himself to go up to the school and hit my son. When Michael came home and relayed the incident, I was HOT. Heat rose up in me like a pot of boiling water over a high flame. If you couldn't see the steam blowing out my ears, you probably would have felt it if you came too close.

My husband knew me all too well, so he insisted on taking Michael to school alone the next morning. Oh! But I made my way up to that school not long after he dropped Michael off. Thank GOD he'd already left because I marched right up to that father and said, "¡Yo soy la mamá de Michael!" No need to mention the rest. However, I can tell you this - that father learned really quick that he and his son had better keep their hands off my son or he would not be able to tell if he'd been attacked by a lioness or a vehemently protective mother. Needless to say, we didn't have another problem out of that duo. I probably would have handled it differently if I knew the LORD then like I know Him now.

Our persistent requirement for personal discipline and wise decisions on our children's part caused us to pull back the reins from time to time as they matured. Our daughter Fatima, an honor roll student, asked if she could get a job at Wendy's fast-food restaurant. We agreed with the stipulation that she maintain her grades. After having the job for a brief season her high school grades dropped from A's to B's and C's. She had to give up the job.

A few years later when she was in college, she asked her father if she could take time off from school to get a full-time job. The decision was dad's since he was paying her tuition. He agreed, and she postponed her education for full-time employment. Thankfully she returned to school and later earned her post graduate degree after

she married. She is now an ESL elementary school teacher in New Jersey.

Like his sister, Michael wanted time off from school to earn money. Since I was holding the purse, I insisted that he finish college and afterwards seek employment. Each child is different so decisions made will often vary from child to child. Michael ended up staying in school and graduating from college with a double degree.

As I raised my children, I was reminded of my grandmother who would go to the ocean to pray and ask GOD for money to take care of her children. Without fail she'd find or somehow get the money that she needed. My grandmother believed in GOD. She believed GOD for all that she needed for her children.

This was the example that I held onto. I prayed and still pray for everything concerning my children and now their children. I pray for my children when they're sick. I pray for them when they're well. I thank GOD for them when they're doing well, and I thank GOD for them when things are not so good. Today I see that they do the same for their own children.

I also see them doing many of the things that they didn't like to do when they were growing up. My daughter didn't like our routine house cleaning Saturdays, but now I see her enforcing the same practice in her own home. I see them serving in ministry in their church just as their father and I learned to do. I see a lot of me in my children and them in us.

I don't have an ounce of regret for choosing motherhood over partying. I'm glad that I didn't sacrifice the permanent (my children's development and security) for the immediate and temporal fun of partying. I mothered so that my children would seek to be all that GOD made them to be. The result of such parenting is that they honor their father and I. Most of all, they live to reflect and honor GOD.

Consistent, Persistent, and when need be, Resistant!

Love

the Changing Agent

Vonnie & Velma

Isaac, who had a taste for wild game, loved Esau, but Rebekah loved Jacob.
(Genesis 25:28 ^{NIV})

Now Israel (*previously known as Jacob*) loved Joseph more than any of his other sons, because he had been born to him in his old age; and he made an ornate robe for him. When his brothers saw that their father loved him more than any of them, they hated him and could not speak a kind word to him.
(Genesis 37:3-4 ^{NIV})

The two of us are sisters. We were raised in a Christian home. But growing up we saw first-hand the destruction that favoritism brings to members of a family.

We are the eldest two children of a woman who was considered insignificant by her very own parents, a woman who was snubbed instead of loved, pushed aside and barely recognized, a woman broken by disfavor, and consequently lived never realizing her true value. Our mother, as talented as she was, never seemed to be good enough to bring delight to her parents as her siblings did.

As a result of her impaired self-worth the two of us were handed over to our grandparents who then perpetuated that same favoritism by esteeming one of us over the other. Though we didn't quite know it at the time, we both suffered from low self-esteem. As a result, the sister connection that we shared was disjointed.

When we were in our teens and matured enough to make decisions for our own futures, we accepted CHRIST. We later decided that no matter what - we would never favor one of our children over the other.

Sometime later we both drifted away from the LORD, during which time we each married and had children. We foolishly walked away from GOD, but He never abandoned us. It was only when we came back to the LORD that we were able to mend our disjointed sisterhood. We found out that our individual identities rested in CHRIST JESUS. We learned that our immeasurable value had already been established by GOD.

I, Vonnie, had two children, a daughter and a son.

And I, Velma, have two daughters.

The three girls were close in age. They grew up like sisters.

Little Benjamin was the prince of the roost. He was ten years younger than his sister Nicole. Since infancy he was an easy-going child. Loving him was just as easy. But he sure cried a lot. Benjamin was speech delayed. I guess some of that crying was his way of communicating, and some of it was because he was a tad bit spoiled (of course, spoken by the mommy who spoiled him).

I was wiser and more mature when Benjamin came along and consequently more attentive to his development. I tried to make sure he had all that he needed for his proper development. We made weekly trips to the speech therapist. I selected his daycare with caution and hired a tutor to help him with his schoolwork. I introduced him to CHRIST when he was very young. I took him to Children's Church, and he attended youth meetings when he became a teenager. There was one missing element - the consistent presence and love of his father.

Like so many mothers, I'm often saddened by the effects that an insincere absentee father has on my child. In spite of it all, I hold fast to Father GOD with the full assurance that my Benjamin will one day realize a father's affirming love through GOD himself.

I thank GOD for the love that He gave me for my children. I thank Him for the love to stand in the gap for them, and them for each other. I firmly believe that the impenetrable love that my daughter and son had for each other was due to my determination to love each without partiality. Nicole was very protective of her brother and Benjamin absolutely adored his sister.

Nicole passed suddenly at the age of 21 after a brief bout with Lupus. During her last days we'd sit together in her hospital room, sometimes just the two of us. On one of those visits she said, referring to her brother, "Ma, I love him so much." Today I know that even in her absence Benjamin holds a special place in his heart for his big sister. Favoritism would have prevented that love.

Now, my two girls were different as day and night. The eldest was head strong and hell-bent on doing her own thing, and the youngest was most often compliant. It would have been easy to choose a favorite, but I was determined to be the end of the line in my family for imposed dissension between siblings. I genuinely loved both of my girls, and they loved each other. They were tight despite their differences. There was no coming between them. Yvette protected her little sister, and Vanessa defended her big sister.

I came back to the LORD when the girls were in their early teens, and I brought them along for the journey. They bucked up against the new me at first, but then they saw me start to live by faith.

Not long after my return to CHRIST my Yvette drove me to my knees and kept me there for twenty years. I stayed there because I loved her and because I knew that GOD had his hand on her. I knew without a doubt that GOD had a specific and unique purpose for each of my girls.

So, what was I to do? I prayed. I prayed even during those times when I was too frustrated to talk and when words just weren't enough. I gave my daughter up to the LORD and tried to go about life as usual, but something deep down inside of me was unsettled.

Vanessa eventually made her own decision for CHRIST, and Yvette chose to lead an alternate life away from the GOD she had come to know.

I loved them both.

Times got harder as Yvette walked deeper and deeper in rebellion. But I loved my daughter, and Vanessa loved her sister. I have to admit that there were times when I was so weary that my devotion to the daughter I loved waned. It was in those trying times that I drew strength from watching Vanessa stand in the gap for her sister. I saw their love. Vanessa protected her sister spiritually and Yvette protected Vanessa physically.

On one occasion when I was teaching a 'Discipleship and Follow-up' class at church, the Lord spoke to my heart. He said "Accept the person, but you do not have to tolerate the sin. Accept her and love her. GOD will change her."

I was not practicing what I'd been teaching. Ouch! I was not supposed to tolerate my daughter. I was to accept her just because I loved her. Tolerating her was simply putting up with her, which is not love. So, I asked the LORD to change my attitude towards my daughter.

On yet another time after I'd been crying out to the LORD for my daughter during a women's fellowship meeting, the LORD specifically said to me, "I have heard you say in your heart "What about me LORD". Well, today I say to you, Yvette is Mine.""

I stood on that word, and as I stood on His word Yvette got worse. The enemy tried to snatch her, but GOD had my daughter in His grasp. Where I got weak at times, His matchless strength was constant.

There were times when the LORD would wake me up in the middle of the night to pray. I'd pray until I'd hear the key turn in the door. Yvette would walk through the front door and say, "Ma, you was praying for me, right?" Even she knew that it could have only been GOD through her mother's prayers that kept her from being killed or caught up in some of the madness she frequently found herself in. I even cried out for her friends. "LORD, protect and save my daughter's friends." He kept them from harm as well.

I heard a message in a sermon one day, "The enemy goes after the precious seed to destroy that seed." That day I reconfirmed my stance. The enemy was NOT going to get my daughter because I had claimed her for CHRIST. I stayed on my knees, and GOD used prayer after prayer to draw my daughter back to Him as He made the much-needed adjustments in my heart.

I prayed, "LORD when you save Yvette let the transformation of my daughter's life be so drastic that the entire Rikers Island be affected by that change."

Sure enough, her decisions changed, and she eventually made her decision for CHRIST. Yvette made JESUS CHRIST LORD of her life.

Well, let me tell you - I watched GOD save my daughter and her friends, many of whom were her coworkers at Rikers Island Correctional Facility. I saw Him break the power of cancelled sin as He transformed my daughter from the inside out.

Today my daughter is bold enough to serve GOD as the *former* President of New York City Correction Officers for CHRIST. And she often takes her sister along when she serves as co-Chaplain of New York's WNBA Liberty basketball team. She also serves as a member of the Fellowship of Christian Athletes.

Yvette has firsthand knowledge of the life changing power of JESUS CHRIST. She and her sister love and serve others in a real practical and understanding way, meeting human needs in Jesus' name without discrimination. It warms my heart to sit and converse with both of my daughters about the things of GOD. My heart is

overjoyed as I see answered prayers unfold before me.

I Peter 4:8[(NIV)] tells us "Above all, love each other deeply, because love covers over a multitude of sins."

My sister and I had different experiences raising our children. The one thing that governed our hearts and home was GOD'S impartial love. It's GOD'S love that annihilates sin; and it's JESUS' precious blood alone that washes away the dirty fingerprints that favoritism leaves behind.

Without Him I could not have been the mother that GOD called me to be to my son and daughter, nor could I have endured the pain of my daughter's death.

Were it not for GOD, my sister could not have stayed on her knees for her daughters. Our family could have ended up with the same dissension that drove a wedge between Jacob and Esau, and the discord that tried to destroy Joseph and his older brothers. But GOD!

We welcomed Jesus CHRIST in with all of His love, and He made the difference in our family. We know without a shadow of a doubt that the value of our lives and the lives of our children is predicated by a loving GOD who desires to shape us as He sees fit.

Mothering by the

Word of GOD

Maldotha

I was blessed to have given birth to five children. Then the LORD blessed me to adopt an additional six children as well as to foster and care for about thirty more over the years. With the help of GOD, I intentionally taught each child, including my grandchildren, the importance of the GOD's word, prayer, and of giving thanks to GOD. I made it a point to teach them the Bible because I knew they'd need to have a personal relationship with GOD and His word in order to overcome life's hurdles and live successful lives.

One of the many Bible scriptures that I taught them to memorize was Psalm 121: 1, 2 (KJV) *I will lift up mine eyes unto the hills, from whence cometh my help. My help cometh from the LORD, which made heaven and earth.'*

This scripture became all too real to us one day shortly after my husband separated himself from our family, back when my first set of children were very small.

One evening after dinner I bathed the children, prayed with them and put them to bed as usual. However, that was no typical night. We had just eaten the last bit of food in the house. I mean, there was absolutely no food left for another meal. The refrigerator, freezer and cupboards were all bare. To compound the problem, I had no money or resources with which to buy food. The one thing I did have was the certainty that despite what I saw or did not see, my children were going to have food to eat in the morning. Why? 'Because my Heavenly Father promised in His word that He would help us. Since there was no need to worry, I did the best thing that I knew to do in a desperate situation - that was to pray.

The children had been in bed about an hour when I woke them up to show them the empty refrigerator and cupboards. We then knelt in the living room to pray for ten dollars for groceries. *Ten dollars stretched pretty far in those days.* My three elementary school children each prayed, I helped my toddler pray, and then I prayed. We thanked our Heavenly Father for hearing our prayer and for helping us. Then I sent the children back to their beds. Again, there was no need for panic because our Heavenly Father had promised in His word that He would be our helper.

Just about thirty minutes after our prayer the doorbell rang. I opened the door to find two family friends standing on our porch. I greeted them both. Neither of them came in. They simply handed me ten dollars each and then left.

These two friends lived about an hour away in Brooklyn. Neither had any knowledge of our need because I hadn't told a soul outside of my children and the Lord, and He already knew the circumstances of our situation.

There are no words to describe how I felt at that moment. My GOD had come to our aid just as He said He would. I was too elated to wait until morning to share the good news with the children, so I woke them up and told them. Together we prayed, thanked our Heavenly Father for providing, and danced around the living room. We had a ball thanking GOD for what He had done. I sent the children back to bed and I continued thanking GOD for sending help.

Several lessons were instilled in my heart that night:

- Fear is unnecessary when you're certain that the LORD is your helper.
- During trying times, my peace will steady my children, which is exactly what I saw. My children didn't fret. They weren't nervous. They, like me, simply expected our Heavenly Father to help us just as He said He would. We didn't know how. We just knew He would.

- GOD'S response to your need will exceed your request or plea. On top of that, He will send the answer even before you ask. In our case, our friends were already en route with the $20 before we prayed for the $10.

Every so often my children, who are now adults and parents themselves, mention this specific moment of GOD's provision. This is confirmation that GOD was not only teaching and relating with me, but He was firmly planting a seed of truth in their hearts that they could pass on to their own children.

This was just one of the many times that GOD stepped in to help us. Time after time, GOD just kept us marveling at His goodness.

Another time, about five years later I decided to buy a house instead of continuing to rent. I searched for a house until I found the exact one that I wanted. It was a four-bedroom, two-bathroom, two-car garage, full basement high-ranch with a large backyard situated on a corner lot, located in one of the best school districts in the State. The only human limitation was that I didn't have a job or the money to purchase the house. It was time once again for the children and I to trust the truth of GOD's word. So, we relied on GOD's promise in Proverbs 3:5, 6 (NKJV)

Trust in the LORD with all your heart; and lean not unto your own understanding. In all your ways acknowledge Him and He will direct your path.

We'd sung this scripture repeatedly over the years to a tune that I made up. It had come time to practice the words we'd sung over and over again.

I needed to find a job in order to purchase the house. I really needed GOD to direct my path. I had never purchased a home alone without my husband, so I needed GOD's direction there too. I just needed my Heavenly Father to order my steps. Once again, when the children and I prayed 'Order My Steps' was precisely what God did.

By faith I took the modest savings that I had and made a down payment on the house. Not long after, GOD led me to a private duty nursing agency where I found employment. There I worked as a Nurse's Assistant at night while I continued to clean houses during the day to earn enough money to purchase the house. All the while and through every obstacle my children and I prayed.

When the time came to close on the purchase there was a gap between the amount of money that I had and the amount that was required to close on the house. But GOD fixed that too. As an answer to our prayers, He closed that gap. He made it possible for us to purchase and move into our new home. I dare not forget to mention that GOD enabled me to pay off that thirty-year mortgage in twenty-seven years, the same time that I paid off a second home that I had purchased just ten years prior to paying off that mortgage. Two mortgages resolved at once; look at GOD!

Our home wasn't perfect. My children didn't have a perfect mother, and I didn't raise perfect children. But I believed GOD when He said, *"Train up a child in the way he should go and when he is old, he will not depart."* (Proverbs 22:6) That's exactly what I tried to do as I aligned my parenting with His word. We studied the Bible daily together as a family and I encouraged them to study GOD's Word for themselves. Rarely was there a day when we weren't memorizing scripture. The routine in our household was Bible study in the morning before breakfast and Bible study at night before bed.

A few of the many Bible verses that I was impressed to teach my children to memorize were: Genesis 1:1, Psalm 1, Psalm 19:7-14, Psalm 23, Psalm 25:1, 2, Psalm 51:7-12, Psalm 100, Proverbs 3:5, 6, Matthew 5:1-16, John 3:16, 17, and 2 Corinthians 5:7, and Psalm 119:11.

We didn't have a faultless home, but it was a good one. I enjoyed raising my children. I especially enjoyed raising them to know the Lord. I knew that with GOD as the Father and head of our household my children would get to know Him personally. On the occasions when my mother would visit, I'd hear her repeatedly tell the children, "There's one thing that GOD cannot have - that's grandchildren. So, you'd better get to know Him for yourself." She'd tell them that they needed to be directly related to the Most High GOD; and that, through His Son Jesus CHRIST. Then and only then, could they become children of GOD.

To GOD be the glory for the lives of each one of my children, grandchildren, and great-grandchild. I am now reaping the benefits of relying on GOD's word and teaching my children to do likewise.

Making Memories

Rossina

We had a lovely three-story brick home in the middle of Oneonta, New York. My husband worked as a professor at the local college, and I taught piano lessons from our home while taking care of our two adorable little girls. My husband's salary at the time was barely enough to cover our living expenses throughout the academic year. And because professors were not paid during the summer, I used the $3 I earned from each half-hour piano lesson to cover household expenses while he was on summer break from the classroom.

My mother and I co-owned a farm about forty minutes from my house. Despite this, my husband and I would often have little to no money or food for our small family after the bills were paid during those lean summer months. Just about the only thing we had was milk from our farm's resident cow, which we'd often use to make ice cream.

I remember a time when the local donut shop would run a special that gave a free dozen of donuts to every customer who received a cash register receipt with a star stamped on it. As providence would have it, I'd get a receipt with the little red star on it the very day that we'd run out of food. This happened once if not twice a week throughout the summers. Some would call it luck, but we saw it as divine intervention. Just

when we needed it most, GOD would always give us a star. The thrill of getting a star and winning the donuts seemed to offset our circumstances. Those donuts served as food until we could afford to buy groceries. Thankfully the girls enjoyed them even though they weren't filet mignon and grilled asparagus.

Some of the most valuable memories that the girls and I share today were made during that season of our lives. It was then that we began our tradition of family teatime. Our first tea party started 7 o'clock one evening while my husband was at work. There was nothing more than sugar cubes and tea in the pantry, and a solo bottle of milk from our cow in the refrigerator. I sat on the floor sipping tea from a tiny tea set with my 1½ and 3-year-old. It wasn't quite the proper tea with Bone China and linen napkins. Nonetheless, we spent the evening chatting as ladies do. The three of us there on the floor sipping from indelicate miniature teacups were a page out of Astrid Lindgren's Pippi Longstocking.

We took turns sharing the details of our day. And as the cups emptied, I dutifully refilled each one

with warm tea from the kitchen. We chatted, laughed and sipped cup after cup until we were sleepy, and our bellies satisfied. We had tea, a bowl full of sugar cubes, and each other.

We were satisfied. I never got overly concerned with the occasional spills on the floor. The girls would spill and I'd simply clean. They were the perfect ladies, and I was the perfectly refined hostess - Pippi style. We absolutely enjoyed ourselves.

Tea and sugar cubes - that was how I was able to fill their empty bellies during those barren days. We never thought anything of English tradition or scones or whatever else. As simply as I can express it, we were just very hungry that summer. But thanks to hunger we started our own tradition. We exchanged English culinary customs for our own. That was the beginning of our intimate and unforgettable teatimes. I wouldn't trade those days for the world.

That lean season has long since passed and we've migrated from the living room floor to the kitchen table. Thankfully the tradition and memories remain forever imbedded in our hearts. I firmly believe that our daily 7 PM teatime and heartfelt conversations around the kitchen table was why I didn't have any trouble with my teenage daughters.

Now that the girls are in their 40s with families of their own, our days are fuller. Nevertheless, we continue the tradition whenever we have opportunity to sit around a kitchen table in the late afternoons or early evenings. Teatimes these days are not as frequent, but for certain just as precious. When we are together sipping tea, we're mindful to leave the busyness of the day behind. We let our time together and moments of reflection melt the stress away. Teatime is one of our simple pleasures - spa treatments for the soul.

Today I treasure the love that I share with my daughters. I embrace the gift of teatime that we continue to share with each other and with dear friends.

My Blessing

Deborah

I'm a new mother, so I can't say much about motherhood other than that it's an absolute blessing and I love my son. Outside of these the other thing I can say is that GOD's blessings are never burdensome. When GOD sends a blessing, He always provides all that's needed to accompany, enjoy, maintain, and cultivate that blessing.

Several months ago, GOD blessed me with a beautiful baby boy during the most unlikely time of my life. I'd recently exchanged employment for entrepreneurship, and business wasn't doing well. My income and savings were rapidly dwindling. To save money, I gave up my Los Angeles apartment, placed my belongings in storage and drove 2,000+ miles across the country to stay with my mother until I could get back on my feet. Niceties like weekly visits to the salon for personal grooming and necessities like putting gas in my car and paying bills had become a hardship. As I saw it, it was definitely not the time for motherhood.

Prior to the extreme times and drastic cross-country move I was a single woman who enjoyed the accoutrements of singlehood. I travelled with very little restraint, dined at the finest restaurants around the country, cooked on a whim, shopped when I wanted to, and slept in at my leisure. Money was readily available. My space and my time were just that - all mine. I had never given single motherhood a first, second or even a third thought. In fact, I was perfectly alright with the notion that motherly instincts were an attribute for other women and not for me.

With that said, my plan was to regain financial stability and enjoy the single life until marriage knocked on my door. But GOD had another plan.

"For My thoughts are not your thoughts, Nor are your ways My ways," declares the Lord. - Isaiah 55:8

Many are the plans in the mind of a man, but it is the purpose of the Lord that will stand. - Proverbs 19:21

One day during those difficult days I was impressed to become a mother to my newborn nephew. After contending with GOD and myself I decided to obey GOD and became mother to a beautiful one month old. With less than twenty-four hours of preparation I instantly made the shift from singlehood to motherhood despite my financial situation.

Whenever I got overwhelmed with thoughts of inadequacy and my inability to care for my little one who embodies a big life, I was comforted by

the reminder of GOD's empowering grace and continued provision.

Here's how GOD is providing: For one thing, He has given me the joy of motherhood, motherly instincts, and an unexplainable love for my son. Through many dear friends and compassionate people, GOD gave me a room full of baby furniture and clothing for my son to wear until he's a big toddler. Amazingly, since becoming a mother I have not lacked a thing, material or otherwise. GOD has provided for all our needs and then some. Because GOD is the Father of my new family, I also know that with GOD I am not a single parent. And because He is a good Father, He will continue to care for us in His excellent way. In fact, He regularly blesses us with more than we need, desire or ask for. He's just that good.

My experience reminds me of the woman mentioned in 1 Kings Chapter 17. During a time of national drought and great famine the widow and mother was instructed by GOD through the Prophet Elijah to take care of Elijah, the LORD's servant, before meeting her own needs. The poverty-stricken widow obeyed the prophet and prepared a meal for Elijah even though she had only enough flour and oil to make a final meal for she and her son.

As GOD would have it, He provided food for this faithful woman, her son and the prophet until He the drought and famine.

The widow took care of GOD'S servant even when she couldn't afford to do so, and GOD took care of her. That's exactly what GOD is doing for my son and me.

Be In The Moment

Carolyn

Be in the moment. Try very hard to see your child's point of view. Your child needs to know that his or her perspective matters and that their viewpoint is actually being considered.

Of course, your child also needs to understand that he/she must respect you as the adult and that he/she is not your peer. Listen to what your child is trying to communicate and be open to the possibility that your mind can be changed. Even so, know that as the parent you retain the right to the final decision.

I was mindful to listen to my children's individual points of view as they were maturing into who they are today, bearing in mind that my stance could possibly be shaped by their individual perspectives.

Our home was like any other. We had our disagreements but there were no constant battles. It was much

First things first
The fear of the Lord is the beginning of wisdom.
(Proverbs 9:10)

like my home growing up with my own mother.

My husband and I established some clear non-negotiables. Anything contrary to GOD's word and wisdom was a hard 'no'. There was to be no disrespect or disregard for the authority in the home. Our children were to abide by the boundaries that we set, whether in or outside of the house. Otherwise, there would be consequences.

Outside of these core values, their viewpoint was open for consideration as long as their perspective was within reason and was not something reprehensible or sin.

I married into motherhood. Like most other first-time moms, I was clueless about the realities of motherhood. Mothers learn as we go. Fortunately, we have GOD's word *(the Bible)* and His Holy Spirit to guide us.

Our son was a vivacious preschooler, and our daughter was a teenager on her way to college when I stepped into their lives and married their father. Simone was nineteen, already a woman in her own right and quite an outspoken young lady. You didn't have to guess what was on her mind. The day I met her father she was standing by his side in the church lobby. She gave me the look of death, as if to say - You have another thing coming if you think I'm going to give you a big smile and hug. She was fully aware that several women wanted to marry her dad. And so, she was quite naturally protective of her father. I was okay with her stance since I wasn't the least bit interested in her father (at the time).

Once Simone and I established our relationship, no one could say a thing off-putting about me without having to contend with her. Today she is still that strong-willed individual who respectfully speaks her mind. She quickly became very protective of me. I can't say enough about my daughter.

Relaying my faith to my children was important to me. As they were growing up they witnessed their father and I intentionally and subconsciously live out our faith.

When our youngest was little there were times when he would tiptoe down the stairs to the family room to watch me worshiping during my quiet times alone with the Lord. I remember opening my eyes to meet his inquisitive eyes. There were times when little Kwame would sit quietly near me until I was done. He was just precious.

He would hear me praying in tongues and ask, "What's that mommy, Spanish?" He once said,

"You just look like you're in another world when you're down there praying." Another time he said, "You looked like you were having so much fun."

He was watching me.

It was around that time that I asked him if he wanted to receive Jesus into his heart. His innocent response was, "Jesus is too big to fit in my heart." At that point he didn't quite understand the significance of salvation. I knew the moment would come when he would, and it did.

The day came when he sat on my lap and asked question after question about Jesus and salvation. I knew then that it was the Lord opening his heart. That time when I explained the good news of Jesus CHRIST, he was able to comprehend it. When I asked if he wanted to receive Jesus as his Savior and Lord of his life, he said, "Yes mommy." We prayed together and he accepted Jesus CHRIST into his heart. That was the ultimate experience. I bought him a Bible and a little children's devotional book.

Then there were times when he'd join me in the family room to pray. My Kwame prayed prayers that were straight from the throne room. His prayers were straight from what he'd been reading in the Bible.

One night when he was about 13, I heard him talking to someone in his room at a time when he should have been asleep. Assuming he was on his cell phone I went in only to learn that he was talking to the Lord.

On one of our family visits to Barbados I watched him discuss and expound on the book *The Case for CHRIST* with his uncle. On another occasion when I picked him up from school, he told me that he'd had a headache in class, so he asked his teacher for an aspirin.

"Mommy, you know what the teacher said to me? She said, "Close your eyes like this and meditate." I said to myself, that's eastern theology, and I'm as far east as I'm going to go. Can I go to the bathroom?""

It always thrilled me to witness his knowledge of GOD's word.

Much like her brother, our daughter was watching.

Your children
are watching.

The day she accepted Jesus CHRIST as her Lord and Savior is forever etched in my memory. She was a college student at the time. As I drove her to school she said, "I really want to give my heart to the Lord." When I pulled over to the side of the road to continue our conversation, she said, "Well what do you expect? Your friends are always downstairs talking about '"Hallelujah! Praise the Lord', and praising GOD all the time.'"

Our children were watching.

I'm not going to lie, sometimes I get in the flesh. When I do, I'm reminded of GOD's word.

Colossians 1:27
CHRIST in you, the hope of glory.

CHRIST in me, the hope of glory, is to be evident to everyone who encounters me. Sometimes I miss the mark. Even still, GOD relentlessly reminds me that He is the abiding strength and invincible love within me and in our home.

Galatians 5:22-23
But the fruit of the Spirit is love, joy, peace, longsuffering, gentleness, goodness, faith, meekness, temperance: against such there is no law.

I exist solely because of GOD. Therefore, I am nothing and I have nothing apart from Him. I am even incapable of loving GOD without Him first loving me. I love my husband, and together we parent with the love that our Heavenly Father has given us.

Whenever GOD is evident in my situation it's simply because He is already welcomed, present, and dominant in my life. As the head of my life, GOD is free to demonstrate His loving nature through me to my children, husband, and all others I encounter.

Psalm 113:9
"He gives the childless woman a family, making her a happy mother. Praise the Lord!"

Our Tender Moments

This might seem insignificant - It meant the world to me to reach for his little hand and just hold him to myself or to have him climb up on my lap and give me a hug.

My heart's desire was to hear his heart, to understand him. I wanted to ease whatever anxieties he may have had. I wanted to be the one he could always come to. I wanted to always be there for him to freely share his concerns, problems, growing pains, and whatever else he thought was important. I wanted him to tell me if someone bothered him at school.

Our bond was something I never thought I'd experience. It reminds me of my relationship with my own mother and how wonderful it felt when she'd scoop me up in her arms, sit me on her lap where I would snuggle comfortably under her chin.

He would go with me to the intercessory prayer meetings at church. When I was sick, he'd write scripture verses and places them on my pillow. It warms my heart to have him even today in his unguarded moments say, "I love you Mamoo" and to still give me a hug and to still ask my opinion, even though he's at the age where he knows everything (so he thinks).

Just the other day he told his friends - were it not for his mother he didn't know where he would be. "She taught me the parts of speech when nobody was teaching me parts of speech. She taught me to punctuate. She got me through school."

Fun Times

The fun times were the sock fights on laundry day. Kwame would start out throwing socks and together we'd progress to throwing clothes at each other.

Then the times when he'd put on his cape and pretend to be the Caped Crusader; we had so much fun. One of those times he captured me and put his little hand over my mouth to muffle my scream. (Something he saw on some children's show) I could hardly contain my laughter.

Our detours to Dunkin' Donuts and GODIVA Chocolates for an occasional after-school treat; and our mommy-son dates at fine restaurants on Manhattan's Upper West Side - My tiny gentleman who was not as big as the chair would pull the chair out so I could sit. So many fond memories, so much fun.

My children were watching. **Your children are watching.**

Luke 18:15-17

"Now they were bringing even infants to him that he might touch them. And when the disciples saw it, they rebuked them. But Jesus called them to him, saying, "Let the children come to me, and do not hinder them, for to such belongs the kingdom of GOD. Truly, I say to you, whoever does not receive the kingdom of GOD like a child shall not enter it."

Proverbs 22:6

"Direct your children onto the right path, and when they are older, they will not leave it."

Deuteronomy 6:6-7

"These words I am commanding you today must be kept in mind, and you must teach them to your children and speak of them as you sit in your house, as you walk along the road, as you lie down, and as you get up."

Proverbs 29:15-17

"To discipline a child produces wisdom, but a mother is disgraced by an undisciplined child. When the wicked are in authority, sin flourishes, but the godly will live to see their downfall. Discipline your children, and they will give you peace of mind and will make your heart glad."

Dear Mrs. Noah,

Today in a world bent towards destruction, I have
for you just a few questions.

How on earth did you do what you did when you
raised your children to honor God instead of living
like the world who all ended up dead?

When all other people were running amuck,
Your family - saved from the flood, was definitely
not luck.

What did it take to keep your three in line with God
above, in light of that catastrophic flood?

'Kids will be kids' is an idiom we say.
What did it take to keep yours from going or staying
astray?

When all hell broke loose and most were affected,
How did you keep you and yours from being infected?

Whose were the methods you chose as your guide
So that your children would successfully thrive and
survive?

Without belaboring the point or overwhelming you
with questions, I love my children.
I want them with me in Heaven.

Please, please, please advise.

Sincerely,
Mother On a Mission

Dear Mother On a Mission,

*I have much to speak, but I'll keep it short and sweet.
As you so kindly implied, successful mothering is
indeed a laudable feat.*

*My dear, I take no credit for the lives of my three
sons. All glory to the Sovereign Lord. It is He who
saved each one.*

*First and foremost, sure up your relationship with
the Lord. Our Heavenly Father, He will direct your
way once you're on board.*

*Instill in your children God's perfect truth. Live it
out before them so they will subdue their emotions by
their devotion to the surety of God's truth. Mother,
diligently instruct them while they are budding youth.*

*Teach them by example to trust and believe what
God says. They need His word in their hearts, not
simply in their heads.*

*Be sure to train them in God's way. If they go, they
won't stay astray. The unrelenting love of Christ will
draw them back. Just pray.*

*They absorb entertainment through the eyes, touch,
mouth, and ears. Lovingly guide their choices
throughout their formative years.*

Be mindful as they select their friends. It's your duty,
Mother, you're obliged to weigh in.

They will frequently say, "I know, I know!"
Just remember, God gave you the final say-so.

Place your children in the hands of Adonai. Despite
the climate and turbulence of the day; no worries,
Mother, God's love will preserve and sway them in
His way.

From the sincerity of my heart,
Shem, Ham & Japheth's Mom

A critical read: Genesis 6 - 8

Love them.
Discipline them.
Teach them.

John 16:21 (NIV)
A woman giving birth to a child has
pain because her time has come; but when her
baby is born, she forgets the anguish because of
her joy that a child is born into the world.

1 Corinthians 13:1-6 (NLT)
If I could speak all the languages of earth and of
angels, but didn't love others, I would only be a
noisy gong or a clanging cymbal. If I had the gift
of prophecy, and if I understood all of God's
secret plans and possessed all knowledge, and if
I had such faith that I could move mountains, but
didn't love others, I would be nothing. If I gave
everything I have to the poor and even sacrificed

my body, I could boast about it; but if I didn't love others, I would have gained nothing.
Love is patient and kind. Love is not jealous or boastful or proud or rude. It does not demand its own way. It is not irritable, and it keeps no record of being wronged. It does not rejoice about injustice but rejoices whenever the truth wins out. Love never gives up, never loses faith, is always hopeful, and endures through every circumstance.

Psalm 127:3 (NKJV)
Behold, children *are* a heritage from the Lord, The fruit of the womb is a reward.

Psalm 113:9 (NLT)
He gives the childless woman a family, making her a happy mother.
Praise the Lord!

Deuteronomy 11:19 (NIV)
Teach them *(God's word)* to your children, talking about them when you sit at home and when you walk along the road, when you lie down and when you get up.

Proverbs 22:6 (NKJV)
Train up a child in the way he should go, And when he is old he will not depart from it.

Deuteronomy 6:5-7 (NIV)
Love the Lord your God with all your heart and
with all your soul and with all your
strength. These commandments that I give you
today are to be on your hearts. Impress them on
your children. Talk about them when you sit at
home and when you walk along the road, when
you lie down and when you get up.

Matthew 19:13-14 (NIV)
Then people brought little children to Jesus for
him to place his hands on them and pray for
them. But the disciples rebuked them. Jesus
said, "Let the little children come to me, and do
not hinder them, for the kingdom of heaven
belongs to such as these."

1 Timothy 4:7-11 (NIV)
Have nothing to do with godless myths and old
wives' tales; rather, train yourself to be
godly. For physical training is of some value, but
godliness has value for all things, holding
promise for both the present life and the life to
come. This is a trustworthy saying that deserves
full acceptance. That is why we labor and strive,
because we have put our hope in the living
God, who is the Savior of all people, and
especially of those who believe. Command and
teach these things.

Deuteronomy 11:19 (NLT)
Repeat them again and again to your children.
Talk about them when you are at home and when
you are on the road, when you are going to bed
and when you are getting up.

Proverbs 13:24 (NLT) Those who spare the rod of
discipline hate their children. Those who love
their children care enough to discipline them.

Proverbs 23:13-14 (NLT) Don't fail to discipline
your children. The rod of punishment won't kill
them. Physical discipline may well save them
from death.

Proverbs 22:15 (NLT) A youngster's heart is filled
with foolishness, but physical discipline will
drive it far away.

Proverbs 29:15 (NLT) To discipline a child
produces wisdom, but a mother is disgraced by
an undisciplined child.

Proverbs 29:17 (NLT) Discipline your children,
and they will give you peace of mind and will
make your heart glad.

1 John 5:14-15 ^(NKJV) Now this is the confidence that we have in Him, that if we ask anything according to His will, He hears us. And if we know that He hears us, whatever we ask, we know that we have the petitions that we have asked of Him.

Proverbs 31:25-31 She is clothed with strength and dignity; she can laugh at the days to come.
²⁶ She speaks with wisdom,
    and faithful instruction is on her tongue.
²⁷ She watches over the affairs of her household
    and does not eat the bread of idleness.
²⁸ Her children arise and call her blessed;
    her husband also, and he praises her:
²⁹ "Many women do noble things,
    but you surpass them all."
³⁰ Charm is deceptive, and beauty is fleeting;
    but a woman who fears the Lord is to be praised.
³¹ Honor her for all that her hands have done,
    and let her works bring her praise at the city gate.

John 3:16 ^(NKJV) For God so loved the world that He gave His only begotten Son, that whoever believes in Him should not perish but have everlasting life.

PS:

For my son's 4th birthday, I asked my friends to send him a Bible verse written in a card or on a postcard. (The postcard was so postal workers would have a chance to read God's promises too.) He was over-the-top excited each time our kind mailman hand delivered cards to him. He received upwards of 32 Scripture filled cards. Over the course of that year, I read the Bible verses to him, and together we learned each one.

Etching God's word in his memory and instilling it in his great big heart is super important to me.

Excerpt from the book
Man-U-Script: the ethos of manhood

Dear God,

Thank You for my little bundle, my baby boy, this Man-child. Once a figment of my imagination, he's now the realization of my many dreams. He's everything and more than I could ever have imagined. What a beautiful child, my baby. He's resting now, swaddled in my embrace, clinging to my nourishment and wrapped in the warmth of my comfort. My index finger is enclosed in the strength of his tiny hand as he holds my gaze in his own. Or is it his gaze being held by mine? I'm not sure, but either way I'm captivated by the essence of who he is and by what he is destined to become.

His eyes, so engaging, fade behind the weight of heavy eyelids as if someone has drawn the shades to veil the setting sun. The cadence of his breathing steadies as he falls asleep. I enjoy listening to the rising whisper of his infantile snore and I welcome the scent of his warm ambrosial breath. This quiet time to play in his brand-new cottony head of curls is my purest delight. Everything about him is tender and brand-new. God, this demanding yet uncomplicated little person is so easy to please. I love him. Thank You.

I'm amazed that at this very moment in time I coddle a solitary life called my son. Though he's my son, he's far more than just my son. He's progenitor of generations to come. I hold someone's father, grandfather, great, and great-great grandfather. I hold multiple generations all wrapped up in his tender loins. I sit here smiling into the eyes of today and tomorrow at the same time. Something tells me that tucked in the center of my embrace is the embodiment of greatness. Something tells me that today I hold tomorrow's benefit.

God, I know he's Your child and that he's simply here on loan to me. But who is this little yet significant person that I waited for with unreserved expectancy, and now wait on as if he were emperor or king? Who is this that I am so privileged to hold in the fold of my arms, to play with, nourish and adore? Who is this little person that possesses a full-size soul and boundless potential? I often remind myself that the only thing little about my bundle is the size of his body, and that but for a moment. Before I know it, he will be the embodiment of a mature man.

This budding and purpose-filled man-child has captivated my ever-growing devotion with the waking of each day. So, who is he and what will he become? Who is it really that I'm holding today?

This man-child's fascinating existence at this juncture in history is no mere accident. I know that he is here on purpose for a purpose. Without a doubt, I hold in my arms a noteworthy individual, one the world is soon to realize.

Tell me, am I holding a time-wised sage, scribe, or world-renowned poet? Do I hold a lexicographer, a master linguist, or multilingual translator? Is he a world-class doctor or first-rate geneticist? Is he the one to discover answers to age old queries about DNA, RNA, and their non-coding sequences? Is he the one to finally find and develop the cure for sickle cell disease or for genetically dominant diseases like Huntington's disease? Is he the scientist to break the code to cancer's malignancy or unearth Your remedy to end AIDS' global plague?

I'm certain that I'm holding a great man. God, is he the Astrophysicist or Aerospace Engineer who will calculate the position of newfound planets or even invent next generation spacecraft for interplanetary navigation? Is he the Architect to design buildings to house Planetary Scientists across the lunar landscape? Is he the Seismologist to develop the most precise seismometers and accelerometers to accurately forecast as never before the earth's quakes and shifts of its tectonic plates? Is he the one to re-engineer the way in which we fuel automobiles and the manner in which we travel? Or will he be the world leader renowned for successfully negotiating peace in lands ravaged by war?

He's my beautiful baby, and his mere presence has tenderized my heart. I wish that I could protect him from all of life's ills. Like any mother, I wish to be sure that no one will ever hurt him in any way. I'd do my best to disinfect his world and place him in a sterile, pristine and problem free environment suitable just for him. I'd even go before him to shield him from life's difficulty and misfortune. If I could repel inevitable pain to keep him from ever being hurt, I'd consider that too. But wisdom tells me that I would only be protecting him from success.

So, through each trial strengthen him. You be his buttress when fierce storms come to knock him down. Take the pain that life will throw his way and use it to inoculate him from unnecessary woes. Help him to recognize and relate to You early in life. Help him as he makes up his mind at each of life's crossroads. With You as his guide he'll choose right over wrong. May he always stand firm, living an unapologetic life of integrity. May he forever walk in Your abounding favor.

Protect him, Lord. You be his continued defense, so that he's never standing alone. Let him always be aware that he is empowered by You, and that he never has to bow to systemic inequities sanctioned against him. Make him a barrier breaker, a unity maker, and a first-rate negotiator. Place in him the offensive strategy that You designed for him even before his forefathers' conception.

We're enjoying him today. We. live with the expectation of an excellent-to-outstanding tomorrow for our man-child.

Architect of Life, shape his character and make him a disciplined man, one who stands on truth and lives by its principles. Tenderize his heart and make him a man of compassion. Help us to form him, so that he's the best according to your intent.

You are a brilliant God, and he was made in Your image. Sharpen his acumen and help him to cultivate his thoughts. Make him a man of reflective thought and a master strategist. Give him the mind to decipher enigmas, and a legacy of wisdom to hand to his children – a legacy that they'll proudly bequeath to their own children.

When people come to tell him he's weak, You be his strength. When danger comes to harm him, You be his security. When accusers come to defame his character, You be his voice. When temptation sneaks up to knock him off course, You straighten his head and steady his gait. When pressure causes him to sink, You be his buttress, and keep him upright. You be his stability and his standard. You be the measure by which he aligns himself. You be the love in his heart that initiates his every thought, word, and endeavor. You, God, be his truth.

We ask that You endow him with good health and longevity.

His father stands ready to hand him the blueprint for manhood, so that he's prepared for the realities of masculinity. We stand together to shower our seed with the nurturing and leadership he'll need to not only survive but to thrive.

Giver of Life, You have placed this tender life in our hands. Now we look to You to help us help him to live out Your great plan. This precious man-child is Your man.

In Jesus' name, we say Amen.

Man-U-Script: the ethos of manhood, authored by Deborah Williams is available on www.QuoniamGC.com and www.Amazon.com

Excerpt from the book
WISDOM for the excelling life

"WATCH YOUR MOUTH!"

Proverbs 18:21(NKJV)
Death and life are in the power of the tongue.

Proverbs 17:27(NLT)
A truly wise person uses few words; a person with understanding is even-tempered.

Do you want to hear something funny? (Well, not so funny) I sat in my office one day talking to a   co-worker on the phone about how much my boss was annoying me. I inconspicuously ended the phone call when my boss walked into the room but continued my rant via email. I feverishly typed, "Tony (not his real name) is getting on my last nerve. If he says another word to me, I'm going to let him have it. He definitely won't forget the moment!" And then I hit send. The only problem was that I mistakenly sent the email to Tony instead of to my colleague. Tony ended up laughing it off and we managed to maintain a good working relationship. But I don't think I need to tell you that for the moment I'd gotten myself into a tight spot.

You've probably heard the childhood idiom, 'sticks and stones may break your bones but words will never harm you'. And, you may have also heard children say, "I'm rubber, you're glue; whatever you say bounces off of me and sticks to you." Well, there's very little, if any, truth to these sayings. In fact, whether deliberate or idle, misappropriated words can hurt. Words can either harm or help, tear down or build up, depress or encourage. Once uttered into the atmosphere, words have a lasting effect. To ensure that we build and not destroy, wisdom dictates that we speak with restraint, carefully considering our words and conversation.

Now with that said, I had a bit of difficulty coming up with a testimonial for this chapter. I literally spent months pondering what testimony to use or story to tell that would best relay the message. And then, I finally realized the cause of my writer's block. My conversations were out of sync with the point I was trying to convey. I definitely was not practicing the lesson I intended to communicate. (Ouch!) I thought to myself, "How can I possibly encourage someone else to do something that I'm not doing?" I had to admit that the words of my mouth and the meditations of my heart were all too often unacceptable to God. I had to repent.

My mind ran across some not-so-fond memories of times when I fussed about my loved one's faults, complained and fretted about situations outside of my control, indulged in idle telephone chatter that went on so long that I started gossiping and speaking negative things into the lives of others. Of course, I also speak in love and say positive things to encourage others as well as myself; and I practice thanking God for all that He does for me. But, since when does clean water and sewage water flow from the same pipe?

Just as sewage water contaminates the pipe from which it flows, making impure any clean water that might flow through the same conduit, so too does negative speech infect the speaker and taint the speech.

And by the way, if the water's source is unclean the water that springs forth will also be unclean.

So, here's where I am today. I'm in the book of Proverbs, also known as the book of Wisdom, learning some reasons for good conversation and practical ways to change the course of my life by the words I speak.

- Psalm 19:14 (NKJV) Let the words of my mouth, and the meditations of my heart be acceptable in Your sight, O Lord, my strength and my Redeemer.

- Proverbs 10:13 (NIV) Wisdom is found on the lips of the discerning.

- It is a characteristic of wisdom to first filter ones words through restraint.

- Proverbs 12:14 (CJB) One can be filled with good as the result of one's words, and one gets the reward one's deeds deserve.

- Don't use your words to describe your situation. Use them to define your situation. Frame your world by the words you speak.

- Proverbs 12:18 (NIV) Reckless words pierce like a sword, but the tongue of the wise brings healing.

- Seek God in order to change the meditations of your heart. Then the words that emanate from your heart and pass through your lips will change too.

- God hears you talking. In fact, He doesn't miss a word.

- Proverbs 10:19$^{(NIV)}$ Where words are many sin is not absent, but he who holds his tongue is wise.

- Quien todo lo niega, todo lo confiesa. (Spanish Proverb) Too much denial amounts to confession.

- You can lose God's blessing by having a loose mouth.

- The words you speak can change the course of someone's life.

- The one who speaks with truth and stands for righteousness is the victor.

- It's true; the world around us can be bleak and full of darkness. But don't curse the darkness, light a candle.

- It's time to go public. Stop hiding what God has done in your life.

- Obedience, prayer and praise will usher in the move of God.
- You benefit when God is glorified.

- A word in season can change the course of your life and the lives of those around you.

- Children have more need of models than of critics.

- God's word is an automatic antibody to whatever the enemy throws your way. So, speak it.

- Encourage yourself until change comes.

- When the enemy is on your trail you'd better learn how to talk to yourself. You'd better have a Word to speak.

- Encourage yourself. Verbally affirm yourself throughout the day.

- Gossip is the art of saying nothing in a way that leaves nothing unsaid.

- Proverbs 14:23 (NIV) All hard work brings a profit, but mere talk leads only to poverty.

- You have to watch what you call yourself.

- Go ahead, try it. Sing when you're in the midst of the painfully frustrating unknown. A soothing song will change your countenance.

- Worship opens the heart of a sincere speaker.

- Sin is anything that you think, anything that you do and anything that you say that does not please God.

- If you're going to learn the language of faith you're going to have to learn to speak as God does.

- Do you find yourself complaining? Well, hush your mouth and count your blessings.

- Why should I complain to you when I'm close enough to God to speak to Him myself?

- A complainer wastes time complaining instead of making better use of time by working diligently through the problem. Complaining gets you nowhere, so stop complaining.

- Stop complaining. You ought to be bragging on Jesus instead.

- Ask God to change the meditations of your heart and the words that emit from your lips will follow suit.

- God may give you an idea as an answer to prayer. So, go ahead and ask.

- Ask prayerfully, not carefully.

- Maintain your confession; maintain your stance. It'll serve a good purpose.

- So often things are easy to say but quite difficult to endure.

- Candor is king, so speak the truth.

- Your walk should match your talk.

- A mark of maturity is the ability to hold your peace.

- You can't take authority over the storm with the voice of fear.

- God's word is sure. God's word is truth. Let God's word be your reality.

Made in the USA
Monee, IL
17 February 2025

12191696R00056